MW00962709

Science Outside

Susan Canizares
Betsey Chessen

Scholastic Inc.

New York • Toronto • London • Auckland • Sydney

Acknowledgments
Early Childhood Consultants: Ellen Booth Church
Literacy Specialist: Linda Cornwell

Design: Silver Editions
Photo Research: Silver Editions
Endnotes: Susan Russell
Endnote Illustrations: Ruth Flanigan

———————————————

Photographs: Cover: Ariel Skelley/The Stock Market; p. 1: Carini/The Image Works; p. 2: Ariel Skelley/The Stock Market; p. 3: L. Kolvoord/The Image Works; p. 4: Jean-Marc Truchet/Tony Stone Images; p. 5: Blair Seitz/Photo Researchers, Inc.; p. 6: Chris Cheadle/Tony Stone Images; p. 7: Suzanne Szasz/Photo Researchers, Inc.; p. 8: Russell D. Curtis/Photo Researchers, Inc.; p. 9: Paul Barton/The Stock Market; p. 10: Paul Kenward/Tony Stone Images; p. 11: David Young-Wolff/Tony Stone Images; p. 12: Peter Beck/The Stock Market.

No part of this publication may be reproduced in whole or in part, or stored in a retrieval system, or transmitted in any form or by any means, electronic, mechanical, photocopying, recording, or otherwise, without written permission of the publisher. For information regarding permission, write to Scholastic Inc., 555 Broadway, New York, NY 10012.

Canizares, Susan, 1960-
Science outside/Susan Canizares, Betsey Chessen.
p. cm. -- (Learning center emergent readers)
Summary: Simple text and photographs explore the world of science outdoors and how it can involve observing, experimenting, and testing.
ISBN 0-439-04604-1 (pbk.: alk. paper)
1. Science--Study and teaching (Elementary)--Juvenile literature.
2. Nature study--Juvenile literature. [1. Science. 2. Nature study.]
I. Chessen, Betsey, 1970-. II. Title. III. Series.
LB1585.c254 1998
372.3'57044--dc21
98-45009
CIP AC

Copyright © 1999 by Scholastic Inc.
Illustrations copyright © 1999 by Scholastic Inc.
All rights reserved. Published by Scholastic Inc.
Printed in the U.S.A.

4   5   6   7   8   9   10   08   03   02   01   00

What is science outside?

Science is looking

and observing.

Science is experimenting

and testing.

Science is exploring

and discovering.

Science is watching

and waiting.

Science is writing

and recording.

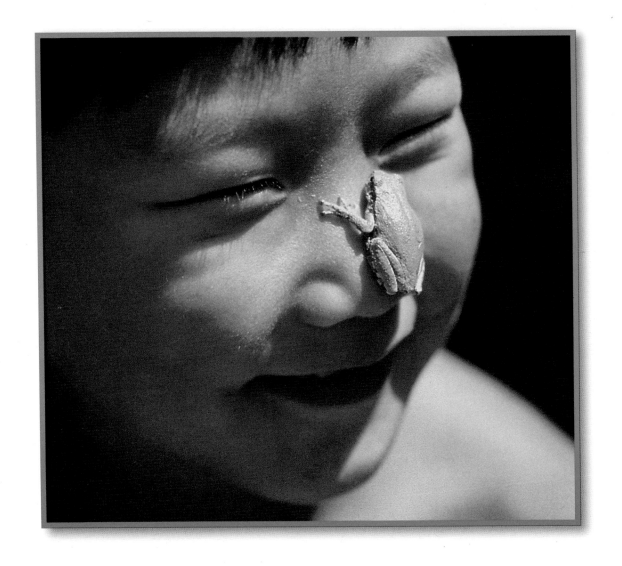

Science outside is fun!

Science Outside

Science is all around us, indoors and out. Science doesn't happen only in school or in big laboratories. And you don't have to be a professional to think like a scientist and do scientific experiments. You already have the basic tools that scientists use—your senses! Scientists use their senses very carefully. Sometimes they also use tools. They work in a specific way called the scientific method. You can use this method, too, and be a scientist in your own backyard. Here are some important parts of the process to remember:

Looking and observing Science begins with looking and observing. Focused attention helps you see details and take in lots of information. Scientists are very good observers. A magnifying glass helps us observe by making tiny things look bigger. Magnifying glasses allow us to see things we might not notice without them, like the intricate pattern on a turtle's shell, the texture of its skin, or the way its eyes blink. Binoculars are used to observe things that are too far away to be seen clearly. They are helpful for watching animals like deer or birds without disturbing them. Binoculars make things appear closer than they are.

Experimenting and testing Careful observations make you think of big questions. Are bubbles always round? Does that beetle eat plants or other insects? If you've made careful observations, you might have some good guesses. In science, a good guess is called a hypothesis. After you make a hypothesis, you set up an experiment to see if you are correct. To test your bubble hypothesis, you might make a square bubble blower to see what shape comes out. For the beetle, you could experiment by placing a small insect and a juicy leaf inside the bug box. Which one does the beetle eat? Designing experiments that produce just the right information is a big challenge in science. You might be surprised by what you find!

Exploring and discovering Exploring also leads to asking questions. Sometimes the question comes first and then exploring reveals the answer. The two boys exploring the cave are using a flashlight to help them collect information. With the light it provides, they may be able to see colors they couldn't see in the dark, find evidence that an animal has been there, or maybe even discover a stalactite! You don't always know what you'll discover. New discoveries can lead to more questions and more experimenting.

Watching and waiting Watching means paying attention to something for a long time. This is an important way to observe changes, notice patterns of behavior, or discover a chemical reaction that may take days to happen. The girl who is watching the caterpillar must look very carefully. She may be counting the number of legs it has or observing how it will respond to her touch. The boy with the jar is waiting to see what may happen to the lizard. Will the lizard change color? Maybe it is ready to shed a layer of skin. You need patience to make the kinds of careful observations that science requires.

Writing and recording Scientists often keep a lab book, or journal. They begin by writing down their observations. You can use a journal to write words about what you notice. Observations can also be recorded by drawing. Scientists often draw what they see and write down a question brought up by their observations. After that, they write their hypothesis—their best-guess answer to the question. Then they write down an experiment to prove the hypothesis. The exact results of the experiment are recorded next. That is called the data. Finally, the scientist draws a conclusion about what has happened and what has been learned. Keeping a lab book that contains this information about each experiment is an important part of the scientific method.

Science is fun! Learning to observe your world the way a scientist would is a valuable way to stir up your curiosity, challenge your senses, increase your skills, and extend your knowledge. Besides, science holds a lot of fun surprises!